# The Virtual Job Guide for the Unemployed

## A Practical Guide to Employment Online

T. Z. Haamid

# Table of Contents

# Introduction

With widespread unemployment and many people seeking jobs, is it any wonder that the economy is in turmoil.   Almost daily there is someone grinding the pavement looking for work and unsure about their future. Knowledge is one thing, but if you cannot use it to make a living for yourself it is pretty much useless.

The state of the economy has its part in creating unemployment in our world. With the lack of financial stability, many companies have laid off workers who relied on their jobs to support themselves and their families. With the lack of jobs, there is less spending on consumer products and sales begin to decrease, and the whole cycle of job losses continues.

What if there was a better way that is sitting right under your nose?   You use it daily and don't think much about the income potential you can gain from it. I am talking about your computer. Knowledge is widespread; you just have to know where to look and how to access it.

The purpose of this eBook is to help people who are unemployed at the moment to find work that is both profitable and enjoyable. They will be able to work virtually, from anywhere they choose, and not be tied to an office or business establishment for hours taking time away from their families and friends.

This trend is growing in the virtual world of work.   According to some statistical data collected 9 to 10 years ago by the Dieringer

Group:

- According to The Dieringer Research Group in a 2004 Interactive Consumer Survey, in 2003 4.4 million workers were telecommuting from home using broadband. That number increased to 8.1 million in 2004 which is an 84% increase in telecommuting workers.

That is a whopping increase in people working from home online. This is proof positive that this trend is not going away any time soon.

Now Jump ahead into the not too distant future. This prediction was made available by Forbes.com in an article written by John Meyer, then CEO of Arise Virtual Solutions in 2012:

- "Working virtually isn't new, but it's growing rapidly. By 2016, just four years from now, 63 million Americans will be working this way, up sharply from 2010's 34 million, according to Forrester Research"

As you can see from these few statistics, the virtual job market is continuing to grow, offering more and more employment opportunities than ever before. There are actually people that have been doing this for a while now, so it is not a myth as some have been led to believe.

Taking things into perspective, it only serves to show that this trend is quickly becoming the norm in the job search arena, and there are dedicated websites that hire people to do virtual work coming online every day.

With that being said, use this guide to your advantage.   Take what knowledge you can from it and good luck in your virtual job search.

## What Does Virtual Employment Mean To The Unemployed?

Many are not aware of the true potential of the computer and especially the Internet. For those who are aware of their capabilities, the opportunities are endless.

A few short years ago, the Internet was only an idea that existed in the mind of the Inventor.

Now, it has become a vast storehouse of knowledge and opportunities for many. Most households have some form of electronic device that has access to the Internet, and many of them have computers. Computers are becoming and have become as common as the television with more and more households logging on to the Internet each day.

But what does all this mean for the workforce that has been displaced from their jobs with no viable source of income in their immediate future? What can the unemployed work force do if there are no jobs in their area, or the jobs have been outsourced to another country?

Some have uprooted and moved their families from communities that they loved to find work in other areas. Others search for jobs through classified ads or job websites where there is much competition for the same position.

But, there is a new job market available to the masses of unemployed workers that is not talked about very much, and you won't find it too often in the media either. It is a job market that does not require you to make a major move unless you choose to. It does not require you to pound the pavement or even consult your local classifieds, although you may find hints of it in the employment section of the local paper. It is a new job market that has been open to people for a while now and only becoming more and more popular as an alternative to traditional jobs.

What I am referring to is virtual employment, where you're working remotely from your home office or local coffee shop, weather via laptop, ipad, or other device capable of Internet access and downloading and uploading documents. There are a few things you will need to be fully ready to join this virtual workforce and these are:

- A computer
- An Internet connection
- An email account
- A phone or communication medium such as Skype
- Software for document processing such as Microsoft Word, Excel, or software provided by the company you work for

This is only some of the equipment and software that make working at home possible. If other items are needed, your new employer will let you know and perhaps provide the resources to obtain them. But, much of what you need is contained online, thus the term virtual work.

# The Electronic Economy and the Virtual Job Market

It would seem that our world is leaning toward becoming a virtual society and the traditional way of doing things are becoming part of the past.

The advent of social media has changed how we relate with others and reshaped our social lives. We find ourselves sharing more life events online, along with photos, witty comics and the like. These things have not only enhanced our social skills but created a platform for a huge network of friends and family unlike in the past. This new type of networking has vast potential for not only people, but businesses alike that are now using social media to reach out to more and more potential customers.

But what about the economic situation in our present world?

It seems that as we dabble in social media and other networking opportunities our economic situation is slowly eroding.

This is not the case with the Internet and E-Commerce. The Electronic Economy is alive and well and according to statistics just keeps growing.

According to statistics from statista.com, in 2002, online business to consumer retail sales were at $72 billion and has only increased over the years.

"The statistic shows U.S. e-commerce sales from 2000 to 2013. In 2012, B2C online retail sales spending in the United States amounted to 289 billion U.S. dollars, a 13 percent growth from the previous year. Online B2C sales recovered continued to grow to 322 billion U.S. dollars in 2013, the majority of which were accumulated through retail e-commerce sales that year."

This information shows us that the economy is in fact growing and prospering in the online world, and this says a lot about online jobs and the virtual workforce, which is also growing and gaining in popularity among workers who prefer to work at home.

Many of these workers have their own businesses online, while others work for companies that outsource their work to potential hires. Either way, consumers businesses, and workers all profit from these digital trends.

Many companies have downsized their workforce in the office and increased their workforce online. The transition is not something that they advertise heavily. Those in the know go about applying for jobs online with virtual employers and continue their lives quietly at home, enjoying the many benefits of time freedom and flexibility in their working life. What they gain is greater than any benefit they would find in a traditional job.

So the trend is while the traditional economy is faltering, the electronic economy is growing and thriving. While traditional jobs are becoming scarce, virtual work is increasing and workers are prospering.

From this we can gather that our world and

society are making a rapid transition to becoming a more digital world. This will allow individuals more time freedom to spend with their family and friends, more ways to make money from home, and even more ways to spend it. This is the new Internet economy and workforce of the future.

## Go Where the Jobs Are

It only stands to reason that if you are unemployed to go where the jobs are being offered. In this case, you will do an online search for "virtual jobs" or "virtual jobs online" "virtual companies that are hiring" and similar search phrases. These should yield some starting results that you can research and see if they are a match for what you may be looking for.

If you have certain skills that are easily converted to the online environment, then by all means search for those types of jobs highlighting those skills. It could be data entry, bookkeeping, medical transcribing, virtual assistant, or even writing.

In your online search, you may be required to apply through email or by submitting an online resume or cover letter through the website. Always make sure that you double check everything before submitting to these mediums because once they are submitted, you can't get them back. Ensure that you highlight your knowledge and skills related to the job being offered.

Take notes on which websites you have applied to and what the results were. Or to save time you can just bookmark the site and go back to it for reference at a later time.

Make an effort to send an inquiry into the application process; this lets the employer know that you are still interested in the position. Remember, even though you may not be face to face with the potential employer, how you conduct yourself through your emails and online speaks volumes about the type of worker you will be.

If you need some more ideas on the types of virtual work you can apply for, here is a list of the 10 top-paying virtual jobs from forbes.com (thinking out of the cube):

- **Teleradiologist**
Estimated Annual earnings $100,000 to $400,000

Estimated Hourly earnings $80
- **Telepharmacists**

Estimated Annual earnings $112,000

Estimated Hourly earnings $54
- **Telenurses**

Estimated Annual earnings $65,000

Estimated Hourly earnings $31
- **Technical Writers**

Estimated Annual earnings $63,000

Estimated Hourly earnings $30
- **Online Post-Secondary Teachers**

Estimated Annual earnings $62,000
- **Translators**

Estimated Annual earnings $43,000

Estimated Hourly earnings $21
- **Phone Sex Operators**

Estimated Annual earnings $40,000

Estimated Hourly earnings $20
- **Virtual Tax Preparers**

Estimated Annual earnings $39,000

Estimated Hourly earnings $19
- **Medical Transcriptionists**

Estimated Annual earnings $33,000

Estimated Hourly earnings $16
- **Customer Service Representatives**

Estimated Annual earnings $30,000

Estimated Hourly earnings $15

Now that you know there are employment

opportunities online and it is not a myth or bogus claim, let's begin to prepare the way for obtaining one of them, and begin the transition into working online for your future employer.

# The Success Mindset

If you think you can do a thing or think you can't do a thing, you're right.
-Henry Ford

Success is a state of mind; your thought life dictates your outer life. So it goes with success. If you think you can be successful you will be successful eventually, if you think you can't you won't.

If you truly want to be successful you need to develop the success mindset. There are volumes of material written on the subject of success, with many techniques that you can use to lead you in the direction you want to go.

The basics of the success formula are well known and many have applied them to their lives and have reaped great rewards. If you want a virtual job you have to get into the mindset of being a virtual worker. This means that you must be motivated to do your best.

If there are certain skill sets that you lack knowledge in, take some courses to get the skills you need. Say for example, you don't know much about word processing software, there are free courses available online that can teach you how to operate this software. You may even have a learning program on your computer related to the software that it contains. Use the resources available to you and you will be successful.

This section will provide you with some tips to help you develop a success mindset. These techniques are not all inclusive but they provide the basic steps you need to take to begin your journey on the road to success.

Here are six steps that many successful people have taken on their path to achievement:

## 1. Set some goals
Successful people always set goals that have a specific deadline. Such as I will lose 20 pounds in 90 days, they do not say I will lose weight at

some point this year. That is not very specific. Always make sure to set specific and concrete goals that have a deadline for completion if you want to accomplish them.

## 2. Get started right away

Successful people don't put off tomorrow what they can do today. Start right away on achieving your goals, and you will begin the process of momentum in your journey. They don't do everything at once but they take a big step initially and continue to take small steps toward reaching the ultimate prize. They may mark specific dates on the calendar for milestones, or they may ask a friend to hold them accountable for achieving their goal. They do whatever it takes to keep going, but they start and take action, and that is the most important thing.

## 3. Use positive thinking

The successful person is the eternal optimist; they see the positive in situations that others may think is impossible.    They do not live with their head in the clouds but are practical and use every situation as a stepping stone to achieve their goals. They believe in themselves and their ability to reach great heights and to achieve the goals they have set out for themselves.

## 4. Take action
While many would wait around to see if they can collect all the data before making a decision, the successful person takes the basic elements they need and take action right away. They do not make decisions blindly but they also do not wait around analyzing the situation to the point of paralysis either.   All they need is the basic outline of a situation, the important things they need to know and they go from there.

## 5. Be determined
Not knowing the final outcome is okay. The best laid plans do not always go the way we imagine they will. The best thing you can do is to not let the little bumps in the road detract you away from your goal. Stick to it no matter what; be determined to reach your goal and no matter how things unfold keep your end vision in sight and you will get there.

## 6. Attract what you want
There are many people who have used the law of attraction to become successful. What they have done is envision their goals clearly in their minds and used their thoughts to attract

what it is they desire most. What you think about becomes reality. Success is not something that is random and happens randomly to people, they make it happen. If you follow these steps you will be on the path to success.

# Building a Reputation in the Online World

Your success depends on your reputation. It can either be positive or negative. The online world may not be as forgiving as the outer world because what footprints you leave on the Web are there for everyone to see. What you choose to identify with in your social media accounts says a lot about you as a person. Make a good impression of yourself in the online world and it will carry you far.

You are known by what you post online to social media.   If you post something negative and people read it, they may get the wrong impression about you.   It could be that you were angry or upset and posted something personal about yourself or someone else that had a lasting effect. Try to make sure that when you post to your social media accounts, blogs, forums, or anywhere on the Web make sure that it is something that is positive and reflects your best self.

Building a good reputation reaps many benefits; others may seek you out if you have branded yourself as an expert in your field. You can use your social media accounts or other types of sites to build your career and network with other professionals. Be known for what you know about a subject or field. Try to stay away from posting anything negative or personal other than basic information that the reader may benefit from.

If you post videos online, make sure that they reflect your best self and that you are not using it to make someone else look bad. Believe it or not potential employers do a little background check into your social media and online reputation. If they see negative or offensive posts, they may get the wrong impression about you and decide not to hire you for the job.

Keep it clean, keep it positive and you can't go

wrong. It is just as in life; you want to make a good first impression to an employer so they see your value to their company and don't mind having you work for them if you display quality characteristics. Manage your virtual reputation responsibly.

# How to Conduct Telephone and Online Interviews

Conducting a telephone or online interview is a bit different than in-person interviews. There are ways to prepare and these tips should help you be successful and may land you the job of your dreams.

Telephone Interview Tips:

- **<u>Use a landline phone.</u>** Don't risk having your call dropped in the middle of the interview if you are using a cell phone service. It can be irritating to both you and the potential employer if the call is constantly breaking up or they can't hear you because you don't have good reception. If you must use a cell phone because you don't have a landline, make sure that you go to an area that has good reception so you don't have to worry about your calls being dropped.

- **<u>Have all your materials in hand.</u>** You can lay out your resume, cover letter, and notes about your objective so that you can easily locate them when you are asked questions. You want to have your career objective clearly stated in case this was not included in your original cover letter or resume. Also have a pen and pad of paper handy to take notes during the interview and anything else you may feel you need. Because you are not face to face with the potential employer you can have anything in front of you that helps you be successful in the interview.

- **<u>Eliminate distractions.</u>** Make sure that you find a quiet area in your home to conduct the interview and stay there. If you can, strive to have the interview time set at a definite time so you can prepare and avoid interruptions. If you have young children this can be challenging as they require a lot of attention, but you can make arrangements to have someone babysit them while you are in your interview. Make sure that they are fed and given activities to do while you are on the phone.

- **<u>Speak slowly and clearly.</u>** During your interview, speak more slowly and try to enunciate your words clearly. Telephone interviews are challenging because you are not face to face where you can see the person's face and see them speak. If you are having a difficult time hearing your potential employer over the phone, kindly and politely let them know that you are having trouble understanding them.

- **<u>You can't be seen by the interviewer.</u>** Remember that you can't be seen by the interviewer so they cannot read any body language that you may project. This is why it is important to be aware of jokes or sarcastic remarks as they may be interpreted differently over the phone. Stays focused on the task at hand and only provide information that gives you the best chance of getting the job.

- **<u>Don't eat, drink or chew gum.</u>** This

goes without saying. It can be very unprofessional during your phone interview and give the employer a less than favorable impression of you if you are popping food into your mouth and trying to speak. Do eat before your interview so that you can focus and be at your best.

- **<u>Prepare your questions in advance.</u>** Just like a face to face interview, make sure that you have your questions written down that you want to ask the employer at the end of the interview. Do not concern yourself too much with salary and only mention it if the interviewer does. Focus your questions on how the company works, what the position entails, and what are their expectations of their employees.

Now that you have a better idea of how to conduct a telephone interview, let's move on to the virtual world and how to conduct an interview online. Here are a few more tips.

Online Interview Tips:

- **<u>Make sure your technology is functioning correctly.</u>** Before your interview be sure that the technology you will be using for your virtual interview is installed and functioning properly. You will need to test your Internet connectivity and also have a web cam and microphone set up so things go smoothly. The worse thing for this type of interview is to have problems with the technology during the interview process. It makes you look unprofessional and your potential employer might wonder if you have the skills to do the job if you cannot even set up your technology right. It looks doubtful that you want the job or that you can even do it especially if it is a technical job you are applying for.   Also, during the interview do not make reference to how weird it is doing an interview online or how surreal it is. You will appear inexperienced if you do, so act as if you have done it a million times.


- **<u>Preparing the Environment.</u>**   Before the interview set up your environment to reflect professionalism.   Position your computer and webcam so that the background is a blank wall, or other professional setting.   Things like bookshelves and professional decor should be highlighted. Make sure there is no background noise and turn off the television and radio. Also, make sure that children and pets do not make unexpected appearances during your interview. Your potential employer may not appreciate the distractions.

- **<u>Dress Successfully.</u>** For your virtual interview, dress in the same way that you would if you were meeting your potential employer face to face. If you are not sure what type or style of attire to wear, ask the human resources department what would be best. Do not wear bright or bold colors as they tend to be distracting. Also do not wear gaudy jewelry. You want your interviewer to notice you, not what you are wearing.

- **<u>Position Yourself as a Winner.</u>** Since you are not in a face-to-face interview you body language is still very important, so manage it in your virtual interview. You should sit up straight and maintain eye contact with the interviewer by looking directly into the webcam. Do not fidget, slouch or yawn during your interview. Some programs that your interviewer uses may have a recording feature, this means that if you slip up it can be rewound and viewed over and over again so take care in how you present yourself.

- **Practice Before the Interview.**  You should do a trial run of the interview before the big day. Enlist the help of a trusted friend or family member to do a mock interview with you and use the equipment that you will be using in the interview. Ask them how you appear on camera, if the lighting is sufficient, do you appear professional and is the sound quality good. All these things should put your mind at ease so you can focus during the actual interview process.

- **Do Show And Tell.**  In person interviews are very different than virtual ones. The interviewer can pick up on a lot more if they are face to face with you, but this is not the case if you are doing a virtual interview. Enthusiasm and interest must be told to the interviewer.   Do some research on the company before the interview and relay to the interviewer why you would be the best candidate for the job. Since you are miles apart you will need to tell them about your enthusiasm and show it with the tone of your voice and facial expressions. Tell them about your qualifications, skills and experience and why you feel you deserve the job.

- **<u>Get It Right and Take Your Time.</u>** You should practice your responses to possible questions the interviewer may ask you. You will want to do this in a clear and precise tone and using your best verbal communication skills. Use proper grammar in your sentences and avoid using "ums" and "ahs" during your interview. If you are required to type some of your responses, do pay attention to grammar and spelling. Do not use any abbreviations, such as "ppl" for people or "thx" or "ty" for thank you.

- **<u>Be True To Yourself.</u>** Virtual interviews give employers a quick clip of who you are, though it is not in depth they can determine through a short interview online whether you are a good match for their company. Do not try to be the person you think the interviewer wants but be true to yourself, just be you. Focusing on being the best person you are capable of being scores higher in the sight of the interviewer. The more authentic you are, and present what you have to offer that is unique to you, the better your chances of gaining the interviewers confidence. This may lead to a second interview and eventually a hire.

# The Winning Cover Letter and Resume

Cover letters and resumes are your sales materials that you give to sell yourself to potential employers. You sell yourself and your abilities through highlighting your skills, potential, attitude and experiences. Not all cover letters and resumes do the job they were intended to do because many lack the skills to create them properly. You may hire a resume service to write your cover letter and resume which can save you time but it does cost. This is more of a personal choice, and it is up to each individual how they choose to approach this subject.

If you are going to write your own cover letter and resume, then these tips should help you to develop one that give you the best chance of getting your foot in the door for an interview.

Here are 6 tips on writing a cover letter that gains attention:

1. **Don't just repeat what is in your resume.** In order to stand out from the crowd of potential applicants it is important that your cover letter shows personality, infuse it with some curiosity and interest in the position you are applying for. You may want to talk about advances in the field, a little bit about the history of the industry and how you hope to be a part of innovations that are taking place. Also do not staple your cover letter to the resume.

2. **Keep it short and simple.** Use at least three paragraphs and make every word count. It should be about half a page, so skip long introductions and get right to the point.

3. **Don't address it to a specific person.** Since you do not know who will be going over your cover letter it is best not to address it to any specific person. You can use phrases such as "To Whom It May Concern" or "Dear Hiring Manager" If you are unsure of who to address don't specify anyone, just get right to the heart of the

matter.

4. **Use PDF format for your letter.**
Remember that not every computer is
compatible with your own. Some may not
be able to open files with a .docx or .pages
file, but most can open a PDF file without
having to convert it. If you happen to send
them a document that needs to be
converted, it might get skipped over for one
that they can open. PDF also keeps the
formatting the way you originally created it
and that may not be the case with file that
needs conversion.

5. **Never use the following phrase.** My
name is ___ and I am applying for the
position of ___. This is information that the
interviewer is already aware of and it will
make you seem inexperienced.

6. **Make a strong close.** Keep the close
short and simple. Explain why you are
qualified for the job and what you will bring
to the company. This can be done in a few
short sentences. Don't go overboard, any
longer than a few sentences is just fluff.

Here are 5 basic tips on creating an outline for resumes that stand out:

1. **Write an engaging summary.** Instead of the old method of writing an objective, telling the employer what you want, try a different approach and write a summary focusing on your professional skills and what you, the candidate can bring to the business and to the position. The summary will be focused on you and what you have to offer.

2. **Provide proof of your expertise.** These can also be labeled professional skills, technical competencies, or core competencies, whatever phrase best describes the type of experience you have. This is the section that lists all the skills you possess, your knowledge and experience.

3. **Related experience.** This is what employers focus on the most, so highlight and describe the duties you have performed in past positions. You can include what you contributed to these companies, how many years you worked there and not necessarily any specific dates. You will also include the name of the companies you worked for and

your job title.

4. **Highlight your education.**  Here you will want to state the educational institutions that you attended along with the degree or certificate that you obtained.

5. **Professional developments.**  Also list any professional developments such as on-the-job training, any continuing education credits or trade schools and other non traditional establishments.

You may want to add any other section you feel will help you stand out from other applicants. This can include any awards you may have received, and other outstanding achievements in your field.

Remember, that resumes are personal and unique to each individual applicant, however you need to remember to keep the format basic and to the point. Go over your resume and look for any grammatical and spelling errors, as well as typos. Put the finishing touches to it and get it out there.

# Choosing Your Workspace

Your workspace should reflect professionalism with a personal touch. When choosing your home office location, take privacy into consideration. It would be ideal if you could dedicate a spare room to your home office for you new found virtual job.

If that is not the case, try to choose an area in the home that does not have a lot of foot traffic and very little noise. If you have other housemates, this can be challenging. Some people choose to do their work in the dining room where they are not alone. This can be ideal if you have established work times where you are not distracted by your surroundings.

Some choose to work in their bedroom, but there is a drawback to working in this location in the home as the bedroom is associated with sleep, and you may succumb to slumber during work hours. If you are dedicated and determined to succeed however, you can overcome this tendency and make the bedroom office work for you.

Some companies have established work hours set out for you while others do not. If there are no established working hours, you may choose to work at a time when everyone is sleeping or out of the house, such as young children being in school all day. If this is the case you can choose anywhere in your home that is comfortable and conducive to working and concentrating.

Once you have chosen an area that you definitely can work in, do not change the location as this can be disruptive to productivity. Try to establish yourself in one place. You can however, rearrange your office to your tastes and likes when something becomes dull or boring. This keeps you excited about your job and working from home.

When choosing office furniture, make sure that it is comfortable and ergonomic, such as the chair you choose to sit it. You may be required to sit for long periods and time and having a comfortable chair can ease tension and back aches. Also make sure the desk you are using is the right height for you so that you are not leaning down, or stretching up to reach it.

# Time Management for Online Employment

We all could manage our time a little better, but when it comes to working from home for an employer or even yourself, it is absolutely essential. There are only so many hours in a day that we can work, and getting the most productivity from that short time is important.

If you need help with time management there are many resources that can help you. To get you started here are some suggestions on ways that you can manage your time a little better for your online job.

- **<u>Have A Separate Office.</u>** As stated before this can be challenging to find a place in the home where you can work privately. The reason for having a separate office is that this tells your brain when you enter it that it is work time. This allows you to distinguish between work time and personal time. It is more challenging to make this transition if you have to have your office in other parts of the home that are less private.

- **Alone Time.**   One benefit of working from home is that you will not get distracted so easily by coworkers.   To take advantage of this alone time you can set designated hours or work, or you can work a minimum number of hours until you reach your quota for the week. If you have a difficult time getting motivated and being productive then the set hours may work best for you. If you are more disciplined and productive then the minimal hours will be best.

- **Set Boundaries.**   Since you are working from home you will need to learn to set and enforce boundaries and be responsible for yourself since you are not being watched by a supervisor. This allows you to have a lot of freedom, but don't get carried away.   If you become too comfortable you may begin to slack off on your work. So learn to say "no" to things when it is work time and enforce your boundaries.

- **Remember to Take Frequent Breaks.** Some people cannot sit for long periods of time and need some social interaction especially since you are working alone. These little breaks tend to energize you so you can be more productive. Go out to lunch with a friend, do some exercise at the gym or whatever you feel will give you the break you need so you can get back to work. Try to take a break every 90 minutes to break up your work day.

- **<u>Do Hourly Self Checks.</u>**  Managing yourself is very important. Since you do not have a boss literally standing over your shoulders to keep you on task or telling you what to do, supervising your own productivity becomes primary.   Every hour ask yourself if you are working at your highest potential.   Since you forget things it is important to set reminders of what you need to be doing.   You may want to set the timer or set reminders in your digital calendar to ring every hour to keep you on task. This ensures that you are on track and keeping busy.

# The Advantages and Disadvantages of Virtual Employment

There are many advantages to virtual employment and some disadvantages that have already been mentioned. It all lies in your perspective and the amount of determination you have to overcome the disadvantages and enjoy the many benefits.

One such advantage is that while you have an employer you are basically your own boss or supervisor. This means that how you use your time is entirely up to you.

There is a sense of freedom in working from home that you just can't get by working in an office or other establishment. You can take breaks when you feel you need them, and not be under any policies or procedures about break time. You will not have coworkers distracting you from your work with idle chit-chat. You can avoid the office politics, and this will reduce your stress levels dramatically.

Some of the disadvantages are that you may get lonely at times and long for socialization. There may be times when you have a question about work that needs to be answered and you send an email to the employer, but they do not get back to you right away. These are only a few things that can be annoying for some.

You must assess whether you are a good candidate to work from home, because it takes certain qualities to be able to work alone and be successful at it. So think carefully before you begin this process. Only you will know what the right type of employment for you is and what your needs are.

# Part-Time or Full-Time: Salary Concerns

Depending on your financial needs you may consider either part time work or full time work. If you want to earn more money, then you may decide to work full time from home. If you have an outside job, then a part time position at home would be best to supplement your main income.

There are many types of virtual employment and each one pays differently.   The top 10 that were listed are some of the highest paying positions in the virtual world. You may or may not possess some of these skills to land big jobs like that, but there are many others to choose from that are less technical and many do not require you to have experience for them.

The pay for many virtual jobs is above average. Where you may get only minimum wage or slightly above in the brick and mortar world, the online world may offer you a bit more because many of these companies have reduced their overhead costs and can afford to pay their workers a little more than the average worker's salary or wages.

Once you are finished with the interviewing process and you have been offered the position, inquire into what the pay will be. Sometimes online employers will tell you how much you will be making up front to attract applicants to the job.

Whether you want to supplement your income or go full time working online is entirely up to you and what your current needs are.

Do not, however, concern yourself so much with the pay that you forget the experience you will be gaining through the position. These are skills that are also transferable in the brick and mortar world.

Sometimes if the virtual world does not work out for you and you have worked at it for a while, you can take those skills you have learned to an outside employer. They may see you as more of an asset because you were able to work alone at home online, and that in itself has value. It shows that you have the motivation, time management skills, and determination to succeed.

## The Virtual Workforce of the Future

Every day as time passes our world changes. More and more technology is being developed to make our lives easier and better than the generations that came before us. So we can only speculate that the virtual workforce of the future will continue to grow, and may become the main type of work available to the masses.

Of course those companies that deal in healthcare and human services and food will remain, along with other jobs and companies that require workers to be on the job site. However, the vast majority of work in the future may be outsourced to workers online.

This means that you can live anywhere in the world and still be able to work. The world of work and how we go about it is changing and we have to be willing to change with the times.

# Tips on Fraud

This eBook cannot end without some tips on fraud in the online world. While many companies that offer virtual work online strive to be honest, there are those who have taken advantage of this situation. These tips will offer some valuable insight on what to be aware of when you are searching online for employment.

- **Do Not Pay To Work**.   This is the biggest fraud going around. A company is offering employment online but wants you to pay them a fee for giving you the job. You should never have to pay an employer to give you work.   This may seem obvious but some have fallen for this trick time and time again.

- **Beware of Web Portals.**  This may seem like a legitimate way to find work, but most of the work at home sites listed in them are scams. Things like online chain letter schemes, stuffing envelope schemes, assembly of crafts and other items. If you find such a portal in your job search do avoid it.

- **Beware of Home-Based Business.** Many of the get rich quick gurus thrive on those who have little knowledge of the online world. They make outrageous claims on the money you can make and offer you a digital download on how to make X amount of millions online. Remember, if it is too good to be true, it probably is. The only ones getting rich are the gurus and all you have are empty pockets.

There are many other schemes and fraud online that you must be aware of. Generally if it doesn't sound right and you have a gut feeling about how wrong it sounds, then stay away from it.

# Conclusion

Now that you know you can basically get a job even if you have run out of prospects in the real world that should be a big boost to your confidence levels. It is the intention of this eBook to get people employed no matter their current situation, and I hope that this book has been valuable to you.

Good luck to you, and welcome to the world of virtual employment.

**I would truly like to thank you for reading my book. I would greatly appreciate if you take a minute to write a review on Amazon. As an independent author I rely on reviews for my livelihood and it gives me great pleasure to see my work is appreciated.**